Contents list

Contents list ....

Introduction to fault 2

Liability and fault 4

   The importance of fault in criminal law 4

   Liability without fault in criminal law 9

   Whether there should be liability without fault in criminal law 10

   The importance of fault in civil law 10

   Liability without fault in civil law 14

   Whether there should be liability without fault in civil law 15

Revision 18

   A general guide to revision 18

   Revision of fault 19

Examination practice 24

   A general guide to examination papers 24

   Writing a discussion essay: staging the information logically 24

   Examination practice for fault 26

Answers to self-test questions and tasks 28

Appendix: Abbreviations and acknowledgements 39

Introduction to fault

Fault implies a sense of blameworthiness or wrongdoing. If you are accused of doing something might say "but it wasn't my fault". You will usually mean that you are not to blame for it. In law, person is not at fault they are not usually liable. Whether you have studied criminal or civil law both, you will have seen the concept of fault. In criminal law it mainly relates to *mens rea*, in tort of negligence to breach of duty and in contract law to breach of contract. We will look at ca and examples in each area. It is useful to compare cases when discussing the level of fault invol as it helps to show how the law treats this element of liability.

Examples

A criminal comparison: In most criminal law the fault element (*mens rea*), is subjective recklessr In **DPP v A. 2000**, a 13-year-old boy shot his friend while they were playing with two air pistols. argument that he lacked *mens rea* was rejected as he must have recognised the risk that some h might occur. He had the *mens rea* of subjective recklessness and so was liable. In **Cunningham** prosecution failed to prove that D recognised the risk that his actions might cause harm, so he not subjectively reckless. There was no *mens rea*, so no liability.

A civil comparison: In the tort of negligence the fault element is breach of duty. In **Vowles v E 2002**, a referee in an amateur rugby match allowed an inexperienced player to play in a sc position for which he was not trained. The referee had not reached the standard expected reasonable person, so he was in breach of duty and liable in negligence. In **Latimer v AEC** owners of a factory had taken sufficient care to avoid the risk of harm from a flood. There wa breach of duty, so no liability.

Examination tip

Although liability is usually based on 'fault', there are exceptions. You should be prepared to di: not only the concept of fault and its importance, but also the exceptions and whether it is rig impose liability *without* proof of fault (strict liability).

Task 1

Choose a case from civil or criminal law and explain the level of fault and how it affected lial Then choose a second case where the decision on liability was different so you can compare t as with my examples above.

I have used a range of case examples and hopefully you will be familiar with many of t However, space is limited because I want to include plenty of examples and tasks, so I have included the full facts. If a case is unfamiliar but you feel you would like to use it to illustrate a you will need to look it up. Most should be in your text book, and all criminal and concepts appear in the relevant chapters of my own books on Units 3A and 4C as well as in the other bo this '*the law explained*' series.

Examination tip

You always need cases and examples to illustrate and support what you say. Where possible refer to a theorist on the area to develop your points. You can also develop your point by a for and against the decision, which shows you are trying to provide a balanced view (see Tasks 10). Another idea is to learn and fully understand cases that can be used for several dif concepts, because you can use the same one in different questions – as long as you chang focus.

Example

We can look at how the case of **Brown** can be used to discuss each of the five concepts in Unit 4C AQA Law. This is a very brief outline, as you may not have covered all these concepts. However, it should give you an idea of how you can use a case and then adapt and develop it to different situations – a bit like judges do with law.

Concept	Aspect of the case that relates to this concept	Mention of a theorist where possible
Law and Morals	Whether sexual violence in private should be regulated by law rather than purely a matter of morality	**Devlin** would say 'yes' because immoral acts undermine the fabric of society, even when done in private **Hart** would say 'no' because law and morals should be kept separate **Mill** might say 'yes' because he believed in non-interference in individual rights, but could say 'no' because he added 'unless doing so could harm others'
Law and Justice	Whether justice is achieved by imposing legal sanctions against certain behaviour even if it occurs in private	The above could be used again but also a **Utilitarian** would want to see the greatest benefit for the greatest number so could argue that this is achieved by banning the behaviour of the minority to protect society as a whole
Judicial Creativity	Earlier cases conflicted on whether consent was a defence to serious injuries, the majority indicated the ratio was that it was not	Where a *ratio* is unclear, later judges can select the most appropriate or can distinguish the case on the facts. **Professor Goodhard** said, *"It is by his choice of material facts that the judge creates law"* Arguably with such a serious crime Parliament rather than unelected judges should create the law
Fault	It was unclear whether the decision was based on the amount of harm or whether the harm was intentional	*Mens rea* is an important element of criminal law and where harm is committed with intent it should be penalised The acts had been consented to, so it is wrong that the law penalised the behaviour. Even though there was MR the consent defence should have succeeded
Balancing Conflicting Interests	The interests of the public to be protected from violence had to be balanced against the interests of the individuals to act as they pleased in private	**Devlin** would say that society had to be protected from evil, as did some of the judges in **Brown**. **Lord Lowry** said sadomasochism was *"not conducive to the welfare of society"*, and so a **Utilitarian** might agree with the decision. **Pound** believed that public and private interests should not be balanced against each other as the public interest will always prevail, as seen here

The tasks are intended to reinforce your learning so do these as you go along. The answers are at the end of the booklet. Refer to these for revision and exam practice. I have included a few quotes where appropriate, so use these too; they show that you know what judges have to say about the law.

Liability and fault

"Vicarious liability is a species of strict liability ... an employer who is not personally at fault is m[ade] legally answerable for the fault of his employee" – **Lord Millett** in **Lister v Helsey Hall**

There are three main areas to consider in relation to fault.

The importance of fault

Liability without fault

Whether there should be liability without fault

We'll look at these in relation to criminal and civil law respectively.

The importance of fault in criminal law

Although the most obvious element of fault in criminal law relates to *mens rea*, there is an elem[ent] of fault within the *actus reus*, and it is also relevant to the defences, where D may argue there w[as a] lower degree of fault. At the sentencing stage, the judge may take into account the level of [fault] when deciding on the most appropriate sentence.

Examination tip

Examiners like to see a variety of illustrations so try to use a range of examples from the four a[reas:] fault and *mens rea*, fault and *actus reus*, fault and defences and finally fault and sentencing. I[f you] have also studied civil law you can add from the examples given in that section too.

Fault and *mens rea*

Most crimes require *mens rea*, so even if D has carried out a criminal act, there will be no lia[bility] unless it happened with *mens rea*.

Example

In **Madeley**, a TV show host took some goods from a shop. He was not guilty of theft as he was [able] to show he was suffering from stress and merely forgot to pay for the goods. He did not inte[nd to] avoid paying so did not have the *mens rea* for theft.

There are different levels of *mens rea*, or fault. Intent is the highest, then subjective reckles[sness] and gross negligence.

Intent is the *mens rea* for murder. This indicates a high level of fault; however, D may be guilty [even] if there is only intent to seriously injure (**DPP v Smith**). Also intent includes foreseeing the res[ult as] virtually certain (**Nedrick/Woollin**) and again this seems a lower level of fault than such a s[erious] crime requires.

Example

In **Matthews and Alleyne 2003**, the Ds had thrown V from a bridge into a river. He drowned. [There] was evidence that he had told them he couldn't swim. Their appeal against their convicti[on for] murder failed as the CA decided that they must have realised at least serious injury was vi[rtually] certain because he could not swim.

Subjective recklessness involves finding that D recognised the risk of the consequence, but [went] ahead anyway. Thus in **Cunningham**, the prosecution failed to prove that D was aware his a[ction] might cause harm, so he was not guilty. At one time, there was also objective recklessness. [When] the HL, in **Gemmell and Richards**, overruled **Caldwell** and abolished objective recklessness [it] recognised the injustice of finding D guilty where there was a low level of fault, i.e., where D d[id not] recognise a risk of the consequence but a reasonable person would have done. It is clear now that it is not enough that most people would see a risk, *D* must see that risk.

Example

In **Jones v First-tier Tribunal 2011**, D had run in front of a lorry and the driver was injured. It had been held at trial that he had no *mens rea* for grievous bodily harm as he had only intended to harm himself, not anyone else. On appeal the CA disagreed and held that someone running onto a busy road must have recognised harm could be caused, so he had the *mens rea* of subjective recklessness. This seems a low level of fault for a serious crime, and was reversed by the Supreme Court. In **Jones v FTT 2013**, the SC reinstated the tribunal's decision that there was no *mens rea*. The SC held that what was important was whether D *himself* foresaw harm, and this was a matter for the tribunal and not an appeal court.

Gross negligence is the fault element for manslaughter. In **Wacker 2003**, the Ds were transporting illegal immigrants in a lorry with no ventilation and most died. In finding them guilty of gross negligence manslaughter the judge referred to **Adomako** and the 'ordinary principles of the law of negligence'. It seems wrong that the civil rules on duty of care are applied to a serious crime. Negligence may be sufficient fault for civil law, but it is arguable that for crimes there should be at least subjective recklessness.

Once a duty is established, whether D's conduct was sufficiently grossly negligent for criminal liability is for the jury to decide. This was stated in **Adomako** and confirmed in **Misra**. This may be difficult, and different juries may come to different decisions on how much 'fault' D has shown, even where the facts are similar.

Examples

In **Stone and Dobinson**, the Ds were liable for not getting help for the man's sister.

In **Evans 2009**, D was liable for not getting help for her half-sister who had overdosed on heroin.

In **Wood & Hodgson 2003**, the Ds were not liable for not getting help for a child who had accidently taken ecstasy.

Essay pointer

When evaluating how far the judge takes fault into account in a case it is useful to find one that can be argued from more than one side. For example you could use **Stone and Dobinson** to argue that the level of fault does not always seem to match the decision on liability. The defendants were of low intelligence and had made some efforts to care for his sister, which indicates a low level of fault in respect of her death from anorexia, but the court found them guilty of manslaughter. An argument on the other side, to say the decision was correct, is that her death occurred due to their lack of care and a manslaughter conviction allows the judge discretion when sentencing, so the level of fault can be taken into account at this stage. Looking at a case from more than one side shows you are taking a balanced view when evaluating the law.

For unlawful act manslaughter, the *mens rea* is intent or subjective recklessness. However, only *mens rea* for the unlawful act need be shown, not for the death. Again, this seems to be a low level of fault because someone who recognises the risk of causing some kind of damage to property could be liable for manslaughter if a death occurs.

Example

In a case like **Nedrick**, where the unlawful act is arson (a form of criminal damage), it is only necessary to show that D intends or recognises a risk of damage, not death or serious injury. In the case, he poured paraffin through V's letterbox so arson was clearly intended. *Mens rea* is there easy to prove for a manslaughter charge to succeed. Again, this seems a rather low level of fau[lt for] a serious crime.

Essay pointer

Both types of manslaughter can be used when evaluating the importance of fault. It can be said [that] the law should only impose criminal liability on those who have chosen to cause harm or we[re at] least subjectively reckless. Gross negligence manslaughter only requires that someone [is] negligent and this is a very low level of fault, especially as it is based on civil negligence. [For] unlawful act manslaughter, the *mens rea* only has to be for the act, so no harm at all needs [to be] intended or recognised as a risk. Again, a low level of fault is seen. The law should focus on the [fault] of D rather than the consequence, but it would appear that many manslaughter conviction[s are] based on what the jury see as a wrongful result (*actus reus*) rather than on D's level of fault (*[mens] rea*).

A final point on *mens rea* and fault is the problems seen with the non-fatal offences agains[t the] person. The *mens rea* does not always match the *actus reus*. So for actual bodily harm the *[mens] rea*, or fault element, is only needed for an assault or battery. Similarly, for **s 20**, the *mens rea* [is] 'some harm' but the charge is grievous bodily harm or wounding.

Examples

In **Roberts**, there was no *mens rea* for any harm but he was guilty of causing actual bodily [harm] when the victim injured herself in getting away from him.

In **Savage**, there was no *mens rea* for harm but she was guilty of causing actual bodily harm [when] the glass accidentally broke, causing an injury.

Fault and *actus reus*

Although *mens rea* is the main fault element in criminal law, *actus reus* also relates to fault. [The] general rule is that D's actions must be voluntary.

Example

In **Leicester v Pearson**, D was pushed onto a crossing by another car. There was no convicti[on for] failing to stop at a pedestrian crossing because he was not at fault.

Causation also has a connection with fault. If another person is seen to be more at fault in c[ausing] the result, and this includes the victim's own actions, the chain of causation may be broken [by that] person's actions. D may be at fault in respect of a lesser crime, but not the one that resulted.

Example

In **Kennedy 2007**, D had committed an unlawful act in supplying the heroin, but the victim's [own] self-administering the drug broke the chain of causation. D did not cause death so he was no[t guilty] of manslaughter. The death was not his fault; only the lesser crime of supplying illegal drugs.

Essay pointer

One problem which can be discussed in an essay is that if someone acts foreseeably the chai[n is not] broken so D is liable for the full consequences, even if not intended or foreseen. This seems [harsh] as can be seen in **Roberts** where no harm was intended or foreseen, but he was liable for ABH. [The] thin-skull rule also seems harsh because there may be liability for consequences com[pletely] unforeseen by D, as in **Blaue**.

Task 2

Using three criminal cases you know, explain the fault element and how this affected whether or not D was found guilty of an offence.

Fault and defences

The fault element can be removed or reduced by the defences. Defences such as diminished responsibility and insanity show a lesser degree of fault in that D is not fully responsible. Automatism shows no fault at all because D has no control over the act committed. In **Hill v Baxter 1958**, a hypothetical example was given of D being attacked by a swarm of bees whilst driving a car. If this caused a total loss of control, the automatism defence would succeed. This total lack of fault is reflected in the result. A successful plea of automatism means an acquittal. Duress and self-defence show a reduced level of fault, although they *excuse* rather than remove it, as you are not saying, "*I did it but it wasn't my fault*" but "*I did it but had good reason to do so*". Intoxication may affect fault if D is involuntarily intoxicated and can't form intent. Voluntary intoxication reduces the level of fault if the *mens rea* is intent only, and any conviction will be for the lesser crime, e.g., manslaughter not murder or **s 20** not **s 18**. However, if *mens rea* includes recklessness, D is seen to be reckless, and thus at fault, in getting drunk (**Majewski**). It is arguable that being reckless in getting drunk is not the same as being reckless in committing an assault, but in **Majewski**, the HL held that it supplied sufficient evidence of *mens rea* for the charge of ABH.

The **Coroners and Justice Act** defences recognise that D is not fully blameworthy in some circumstances. If D suffered from diminished responsibility, as in **Freaney 2010**, where she was suffering extreme stress when she killed her son, the conviction is reduced from murder to manslaughter. The same applies where D suffers a loss of control, as in **Clinton 2012**.

These 'partial defences' do not remove the fault element, but indicate there is a lower level of fault so the conviction is for manslaughter not murder. Therefore the fault element can be taken into account by the judge when sentencing, which brings us to the last point.

Task 3

Choose two defences and explain how they affect liability because D is not regarded as fully at fault with a brief comment on whether the result seems fair.

Fault and sentencing

At the final stage of a criminal case the sentence given will reflect the level of fault. Mitigating and aggravating factors are taken into account, so if the circumstances indicate a higher or lower level of fault this is reflected in the sentence. One problem is the mandatory life sentence for murder, which means the judge cannot take into account any lack of moral fault, e.g., in euthanasia cases. All a judge can do to reflect the level of fault is recommend a starting point or a maximum term, but this is a limited discretion. An example is the case of **Inglis**, where the circumstances were similar to **Freaney** but she failed in her plea of diminished responsibility. She was given a life sentence for murder, but with a starting point of 9 years rather than the usual 15, on compassionate grounds.

In some cases, a life sentence is justified because it does reflect the level of fault. Under the **Criminal Justice Act 2003** a whole life sentence can be given for 'exceptionally serious offences'. In such cases the fault element is extremely high and life should mean life. It has been argued that whole life sentences are against the **European Convention on Human Rights** because there is no possibility of review or release, whatever the behaviour of the prisoner. However, in **McLoughlin and Newell 2014**, the CA held that as the **Crime (Sentences) Act 1997** allows for release in exceptional circumstances on compassionate grounds (e.g., where a prisoner is terminally ill) whole life sentences are within the law. The extreme level of fault warrants the refusal of release or review.

A deterrent sentence is less justified because it often sacrifices the interests of the particular to those of society, rather than reflecting the level of fault involved. It is used to stop re-offending deter others from offending, so a custodial sentence may be given where the offence does not re warrant one.

Finally, as regards sentencing generally, it can be argued that the imposition of sanctions and restriction on the freedom of the individual is only justified when that individual has been at fault

Essay pointer

The following are all questions you could consider when evaluating decisions of the courts regar the fault element, with a couple of case examples for each point.

Should intent to commit serious harm be enough for murder? This is a lower level of fault intent to kill but has the same result. **Case examples: Vickers and DPP v Smith.**

How much real fault is there in cases involving omissions? Failing to act does not seem to inv the same level of fault as a conscious decision to act. **Case examples: Stone & Dobinson Pittwood.**

Should the mandatory sentence for murder be abolished? The degree of fault in murder cases be very different, but the result is the same – a life sentence. The level of fault in a vicious mure greater than that in euthanasia cases where D usually acts in what is believed to be the interests of the victim. **Case examples: Cox and Inglis 2010.**

Should there be *mens rea* regarding the death (or at least serious harm) in unlawfu manslaughter? Currently it only requires that D has *mens rea* for the act, not for the death. seems unjust, as it is a lower level of fault than such a serious crime warrants. **Case exam Nedrick and Hancock & Shankland.**

Before moving on to liability without fault make a note of a few cases you could use to evaluat law as regards to the importance of fault. The following task contains some examples.

Task 4

Look at the table below. Write down a brief criticism of the decision in each case and keep th revision and planning for an essay.

Criminal case	Brief facts	Level of fault shown
Savage	A girl threw beer over another girl and the glass slipped causing cuts	Low. *Mens rea* was for the battery only
Khan & Khan	Drug dealers left a girl in a coma and she died	High. They could easily have got help
Clinton	A man killed his wife after seeing graphic pictures of her on Facebook with another man	High. He showed intent to kill her
Blaue	A man stabbed a girl several times and she died after refusing treatment	High. His violence showed a high level of fault
Majewski	A man got into a fight when drunk and caused ABH	Medium. He did not really know what he was doing

Some crimes do not require *mens rea* in any form. Liability without fault is called *strict* liability. You may have studied this earlier. To evaluate this area, you need to consider how far someone *should* be criminally liable without proof of fault, and, as always, there are arguments on both sides.

Liability without fault in criminal law

Strict liability usually applies to regulatory offences, i.e., offences that are not truly criminal in nature such as minor traffic offences. In addition, offences covering areas of social concern or public health, such as the sale of food and alcohol, pollution and protection of the environment, are often strict liability offences.

Examples

In **Meah v Roberts 1977**, D served lemonade which had caustic soda in it to two children. He was not responsible for it being there (it was put in a lemonade bottle by the person cleaning the pipes), but he was found guilty under the **Food and Drug Act 1955**, even though not at fault himself. In **Harrow LBC v Shah 1999**, it was held that the offence of selling a lottery ticket to a person under 16 was one of strict liability, so a shopkeeper was liable even though he was not present at the time of sale and had instructed his staff not to serve underage children.

In 'real' crimes there is more controversy, as seen in **Sweet v Parsley 1970**. A woman let rooms to students. The police raided the premises and found cannabis. She was charged with being 'concerned in the management of premises used for the purpose of smoking cannabis' under the **Dangerous Drugs Act 1965**. She was found guilty even though not at fault – she was completely unaware of the cannabis smoking. The HL eventually acquitted her and established the rule that strict liability could only be imposed where the Act specifically made the offence one of strict liability. In all other cases, a need for *mens rea* would be presumed. In **B v DPP 2000**, the HL reversed a conviction of inciting a child of 14 to indecency on the basis of this principle, saying it particularly strong in serious offences, D having argued he was not at fault as he believed the c was older. For serious crimes, particularly where a prison sentence may result, it is important mens rea should be proved, so that D is not liable unless at fault.

Crimes of absolute liability do not require any fault at all, neither *actus reus* nor *mens rea*. Exam are 'state of affairs' crimes where D can be liable just for being in the wrong place at the wrong ti

Example

In **Winzar**, a drunk was removed from a hospital by the police and put in their car, which was pa on the road. They then arrested him for being found 'drunk on a highway', and he was convic Here there is not only no *mens rea* but no *actus reus*, as he was not acting voluntarily.

Essay pointer

State of affairs crimes such **Winzar** mean D can be liable without being at fault, or even a voluntarily. This seems unfair so can be used when evaluating the law in an essay.

Whether there should be liability without fault in criminal law

Arguments against:

it is unfair to convict D of a criminal offence if not at fault

it leads to the punishment of people who have taken all possible precautions

it means such people have a criminal record

Arguments for:

it makes people more careful

it protects the public

most such offences are minor and carry no social stigma

proving *mens rea* is hard in many minor offences, e.g., trying to prove someone knew they had parked on a yellow line in the snow, so time and money is saved

the judge can address the issue of fault when sentencing

Although there are several arguments for imposing strict liability, the arguments against are strong. A requirement of fault, at least negligence, would be fairer. This is a low level of fa would still protect the public, but it would mean there would be no conviction without some d of fault.

The importance of fault in civil law

Fault is an element of many areas of civil law. It is seen in contract but is particularly import tort. The word negligence itself implies a degree of fault.

Contract law

Fault is, perhaps, less important in contract cases. The fact of breach is enough and there is no e.g., to prove negligence. However, the party in breach is seen as the one at fault, and so da are awarded to the other party. Any breach cases can be used to illustrate the concept. Also, breach is fundamental, the injured party can not only claim damages but also treat the contract as at an end, reflecting the higher level of fault.

Misrepresentation usually relies on proving fraud or negligence. Fraud is a high level of fault. In **Derry v Peek 1889**, it was described as where a false statement was made *knowingly*, without belief in its truth, or *recklessly*, careless as to whether it is true or false. Negligence is a lower level of fault in that it can include a statement which was honestly made, as in **Howard Marine and Dredging Ltd**, where D was at fault, or negligent, in not checking the information.

The law on frustration reflects the fact that where parties to a contract are *not* at fault in ending it neither can enforce it. In **Davis Contractors**, Lord Radcliffe said *"frustration occurs whenever the law recognises that, **without default** of either party, a contractual obligation has become incapable of being performed"*. So, only where neither party could foresee an event, can that event frustrate a contract, if one party could foresee it, or is at fault, the contract will not be frustrated, e.g., **Super Servant II**.

Contract remedies will reflect the degree of fault by the party in breach. Damages are only awarded for foreseeable loss, as established in **Hadley v Baxendale**. Also, rescission is a discretionary remedy, and will not be awarded to a party who has not acted equitably, i.e., who is at fault.

Tort law

The tort of negligence requires proving D has breached a duty at common law or under the **Occupier's Liability Act**. Nuisance requires proving D has interfered unreasonably with someone's enjoyment. In other words it must be proved that D is *at fault*.

Fault and negligence (breach of duty)

You can use any breach of duty cases to discuss the importance of proving fault. Note that D is judged by the standard expected of the reasonable person, not D's own standards. However, it is recognised that in the case of children, age is relevant and they should have a high degree of fault before being found negligent, this rule was confirmed in **Mullin v Richards**.

Example

In **Orchard v Lee 2009**, a supervisor in a school playground was injured when a thirteen-year-old child playing a game of tag ran into her. The CA held that the primary question was whether the conduct of the child was culpable (blameworthy), i.e., had fallen below the standard that should objectively be expected of a child of that age. The correct approach to liability was that confirmed in **Mullin**. For a child to be held culpable the conduct must be 'careless to a very high degree'. As he was in a play area and was not breaking any rules he was not at fault. It was merely an accident.

In professional cases, D is judged against others in the profession. In the case of doctors, against what other doctors would do. In **McDonnell v Holwerda 2003**, a GP examined a child twice. The court held that not recognising the risk of meningitis on the first occasion was not negligent, but the risk was higher by the second so the GP breached her duty on that occasion. This reflected the higher level of fault on the second examination.

The factors the courts consider when deciding if the standard has been reached also relate to fault. If there is only a low risk of something happening and precautions have been taken to avoid the risk, D is less likely to be found at fault, as in **Bolton v Stone** and **Latimer v AEC**. In addition, if there is a social benefit then even if at fault D may escape liability, as in the case of **Watts v Herts CC** where the fire crew were on their way to rescue someone when the badly stored jack caused injury. This is strengthened by the **Compensation Act 2006 s 1**, which provides that in deciding whether D should have taken particular steps to meet the standard of care (e.g., taken precautions), a court may consider whether a requirement to take those steps might prevent a 'desirable activity' from being undertaken. This means a higher level of fault may be acceptable when the activity in question desirable, such as school trips and sporting events.

Essay pointer

Breach of duty is based on not reaching the standard of a reasonable person, although the standard expected of children is lower and therefore the level of fault must be high before liability is found in **Mullins v Richards**. This is not the case with inexperience, only age. In **Nettleship v West** learner driver was expected to show the skill of an ordinary, competent driver. It can be argued a learner driver is not showing the same degree of fault as an experienced driver would be driving negligently. These cases are therefore useful comparisons when evaluating the level of expected in breach of duty cases.

A final point on negligence is causation and the thin skull rule. This is as for criminal law and can seem harsh because D may be liable for completely unexpected consequences.

Example

In **Smith v Leech-Brain**, an employer's negligence (fault) led to a man suffering a small burn, then activated a latent cancer. He died and his widow sued. The employer's level of fault was relation to the death from cancer but even though this was not a foreseeable result he was liable the full consequences, including the employee's death.

Task 5

Choose three cases on breach of contract or breach of a duty of care. Note the element of fault how it affected liability.

Fault and nuisance

In nuisance cases it must be shown that D's act was unreasonable. This is a lesser degree of than negligence. In **Adams v Ursell**, smells from D's fish and chip shop were unreasonable though he was providing a service, and arguably not doing anything wrong. Fault may be a de factor in some nuisance cases though.

Example

In **Christie v Davey**, two neighbours were causing a nuisance to each other; one by music lesso other by banging trays and whistling. The latter was liable because his behaviour was malicious more clearly unreasonable; he showed a higher level of fault. This case is a good illustration c the level of fault may tip the balance as to who is liable in nuisance cases.

Fault and defences and remedies

Tort defences may indicate either a total lack of fault, or reduced fault.

Example

You are late for work because of a flood stopping all transport. You would argue that this was of God, and you should not be punished because you were not at fault in any way. The same in law, so that if an act of God applies, D is not punished.

This special defence of act of God shows that if D is not at fault in any way there is no liability. only applies in nuisance, but also in **Rylands**, which is a tort of strict liability, or 'no fault' li Thus liability may be strict, but is not absolute as there may be a defence. The contributed negligence defence is where fault is reduced. This defence recognises that D may not have solely at fault, so that damages are reduced to reflect the amount that C is also at fault **Gannon v Rotherham MBC**, where the court held that a 14-year-old ought to recognise the of diving into the shallow end of pool, so he was found to have contributed to his injuries. The degree of fault is taken into account by the judge who can apportion damages under the **Law Reform (Contributory Negligence) Act**.

Example

In **Belka v Prosperini 2011**, C had run across a dual carriageway near a roundabout having drunk about four pints of beer. He was hit by a taxi and claimed in negligence. The judge found that he was two-thirds to blame and reduced his damages accordingly. He appealed, arguing that even if blame was to be shared he was not more blameworthy than D. The CA held that his was the greater fault because, although D had been negligent in not anticipating the risk of hitting someone, C had taken a deliberate risk by running across the road in front of the vehicle.

Consent is another defence, which applies where C consents to the risk of harm. It also sometimes succeeds where it can be shown that C is at fault rather than the defendant. There is an overlap with contributory negligence because if the fault is high enough D will be deemed to consent to the risk of harm rather than merely contribute to it.

Example

In **Ratcliff v McConnell**, a 19-year-old student was seriously injured diving into a swimming pool at his college. He had been drinking but the evidence was that he knew what he was doing. The defence of consent succeeded and the college was found not liable. The boy was at fault for diving into the pool while drunk, so was deemed to have consented to the risk of injury.

Task 6

Choose two defences and explain how they affect liability.

Remedies are intended to compensate C rather than punish D, so do not necessarily reflect the degree of fault, just the amount of damage caused. However, D is only liable for *foreseeable* damage, as per **The Wagon Mound**, so fault is relevant here. The more foreseeable something is, the more at fault you are for not avoiding it, so it seems fair that you are liable for foreseeable consequences.

Before moving on to liability without fault make a note of a few cases you could use to evaluate the law as regards to the importance of fault. The following task contains some examples.

Task 7

Look at the table below. Write down a brief criticism of the decision in each case and keep this for revision and planning for an essay.

Tort case	Brief facts	Level of fault
Nettleship v Weston	A learner driver drove negligently, injuring her instructor and was found liable	Low. She was inexperienced
Paris v Stepney BC	A man who was blind in one eye injured the other eye when welding without goggles and his employer was liable	High. The employer knew he was partially blind
Mullins v Richard	One girl was injured during a fight with plastic rulers and the other girl was not in breach of duty	Low,. Because she was only 15
Adams v Ursell	Smells from a fish and chip shop caused a nuisance to residents and the owner was liable	Low. As it is a normal occurrence and he had not acted with malice (unlike in **Christie v Davey**)
Belka v Prosperini	A man ran across a road and was hit by a taxi. His damages were reduced by two-thirds for contributory negligence	Medium. Both parties were at fault but neither totally

Liability without fault in civil law

We'll look at some examples of 'no-fault' liability in contract and tort, and then consider how liability without fault *should* be imposed.

Contract

The rules on revocation and acceptance mean a contract can be formed unknowingly and so can breached without any fault. In particular, the postal rule can be discussed. Acceptance by p complete as soon as something is posted even if it doesn't arrive, as confirmed in **House Insurance v Grant**. This means the other party may not know that an offer has not been accepte

Example

Geoff offers to sell his car to Paul. Paul writes to accept but Geoff doesn't get the letter. Thi Paul doesn't want the car, Geoff sells it to someone else. Paul can sue for breach of contract, can hardly be said that Geoff is at fault. The argument for this rule is that Geoff could exclude saying that acceptance must be in a particular form, or must reach him.

The implied terms under the **Sale of Goods Act** impose liability without fault. Thus, in **Go Perry**, the seller could be sued for the catapult not being of satisfactory quality, even thoug personally at fault. On the other hand, **s 14** will not apply if the defects were brought to the b attention, or the goods were examined and the defect should have been noticed. This reco that if C is at fault, D should not be liable. In **Wilson v Best Travel 1993**, C fell through a glass while on holiday. The tour operator had not breached the implied term under **s 13** of the S **Goods and Services Act** – that the service would be carried out with reasonable care and ski they had checked the premises and there was no obvious danger, they were not at fault.

Innominate terms look at the effect of the breach on C, rather than the degree of fault by D. This means that whatever the level of fault, if the consequences are serious C can rescind the contract as well as claim damages.

Tort

One area of tort that has liability without fault is the **Consumer Protection** Act. This Act imposes strict liability on producers. This means if a product has a defect and causes harm, the producer is liable without the need to prove fault. This also applies to manufacturers. The defences within the Act allow some leeway but the fact remains that a producer or manufacturer can be liable without fault.

Task 8

The **Consumer Protection Act** imposes strict liability on manufacturers, how does this compare with negligence as regards fault?

The main area of strict liability in tort is **Rylands v Fletcher**. There is no need to prove fault, i.e., C need not prove negligence, merely that something has escaped and caused damage. However, a small degree of fault has entered the law here. Although liability is strict in that if damage *is* foreseeable then D is liable regardless of the amount of care taken, in **Cambridge Water Co**, the HL added that if the damage is *not* foreseeable, D will avoid liability.

The other area of strict liability in tort is vicarious liability. As seen in the opening quote, it is not necessary to prove an employer is at fault in any way. In fact, if the employer *is* at fault there will be primary, rather than vicarious liability. Fault is still an important element, as C must prove the negligence (breach) by the employee. However, it is the employer who is sued, and who will pay any compensation, not the person actually at fault.

Example

In **Phelps v Hillingdon BC 2001** and **Carty v Croydon LBC 2005**, the councils were vicariously liable for the negligence of a psychologist and an education officer respectively. The psychologist and education officer had been the ones at fault (they were negligent in their assessments of children with special needs) but in both cases it was the employer, the council, who were liable and had to pay compensation.

Vicarious liability applies even to acts which seem well outside the scope of employment, such as sexual activities, as seen in **Lister v Helsey Hall**. It may seem wrong that an employer can be liable even though not at fault, but the law needs to protect the victim and an employer is not only more likely to be able to pay, but is also able to insure against such claims.

Whether there should be liability without fault in civil law

So why do the courts impose liability on someone who appears blameless? There is not a great deal of controversy in contract law on this issue. Since the courts created the doctrine of frustration in **Taylor v Caldwell**, there is no longer liability for breach of a contract which has become impossible to perform. Until then it was unfair that a person could be sued for breach through no fault of their own. Possibly the rules on offer and acceptance are still unfair, as the offeror may not know an offer has been accepted if the postal rule applies. There is an argument that in a world of instant communication the rule should be abolished so a person cannot unknowingly, and without fault, breach a contract.

As regards tort and how far fault should a requirement, this has been much debated over many years. The question was the subject of the **Pearson Commission Report** in 1978, and this is a good base for a discussion of the idea of fault-based liability as opposed to strict liability.

The Commission was set up because it was recognised that there are many problems for people who have suffered damage. Fault can be hard to prove and many victims are left without compensation for their injuries. One of the main arguments for the introduction of a no-fault compensation scheme is that the tort system is too irrational in providing different levels of remedy for the same type of accident, and sometimes no remedy at all.

Whist recognising the problems, the Commission felt the tort system should be retained. However, it should be supplemented by a more widespread system of social security, e.g., a no-fault compensation scheme was suggested whereby road accident victims could be compensated from a fund administered by the state and paid for by a tiny increase in fuel prices. Tort would remain as alternative. The Commission also recommended a no-fault scheme for product liability, ultra-hazardous activities and authorised vaccines. The first is now covered by the **Consumer Protection Act** and the last by the **Vaccine Damage Act**, but the recommendation that strict liability should be imposed on 'ultra-hazardous' activities was not implemented – although there are one or two dealing with particular areas such as oil pollution and nuclear installations. Such activities are partly covered by the rule in **Rylands v Fletcher**, but many people would prefer them to be governed by statute, as **Rylands** is seen as unpredictable. In **Cambridge Water** and **Transco**, the HL, although declining to abolish the rule, also declined to extend the scope of strict liability further, indicating that it was for Parliament to legislate. Legislation would be able properly to regulate dangerous activities and provide that insurance is compulsory for people dealing in dangerous materials / 'ultra-hazardous' activities.

There was some expectation that a no-fault scheme for medical accidents would be put forward, only a further investigation of the no-fault system operating in New Zealand was suggested nothing was done in this area. The problems continued to be the subject of much debate. The **Redress Act 2006** (which became law in 2012) may help. When introducing the legislation Government recognised that medical negligence claims were lengthy, slow and costly, with fees often exceeding the claim. They were also seen as unfair, with too many variations in outcome (as the Pearson Committee noted). The **Act** allows for compensation up to £20,000 to be paid without the need for a court action, although the right to sue is still available. The Government made clear that fault-based liability should remain the norm for compensation claims; the scheme voluntary and a procedural matter only, intended to offer an alternative to litigation. However, emphasis is on getting it right rather than apportioning fault and the scheme can help to speed the process of getting compensation and avoid the stress of litigation.

Arguments for a no-fault system:

- Everyone is compensated, though possibly to a lesser degree
- Insurance can be used to protect D
- It makes people careful
- The benefit to society of many hazardous activities (e.g., in industry or medicine) means society not the individual should bear the cost
- It limits the number of court cases, so courts are not overloaded
- The fault system can be unfair as sometimes C is fully compensated but sometimes gets nothing
- Proving fault is time-consuming and costly
- The adversarial nature of court proceedings means it may make a relationship worse, e.g., in employment cases or in nuisance cases between neighbours

Arguments for a fault system:

- The wrongdoer pays
- C is fully compensated
- A no-fault system may not make D more careful
- The conditional fee scheme – 'no win, no fee' – helps C to claim without the worry of solicitor's fees

N.B.: Changes to this scheme in April 2013 do not affect this as they only apply after a case is won (where now C has to pay the success fee)

Self-test questions

- Explain how fault is proved in either civil or criminal law
- How may a defence reflect the degree of fault involved?
- Explain two cases where there was no liability because fault could not be proved
- Use two cases to support an argument for imposing/not imposing strict liability
- What effect might fault have on sentencing?
- How does the rule that children are judged against a child of similar age rather than a reasonable adult reflect the level of fault involved?
- How might the various breach factors affect whether fault is proved in negligence?
- How does the defence of contributory negligence reflect the degree of fault involved?

Revision

A general guide to revision

The first and foremost rule for revision is to start early. Too many students leave it until the minute and then get in a panic. If you take it gently and organise your time properly you will f lot more calm and confident when exam time comes. Make a plan of what you want to cover day and try to stick to it. Don't forget to include some breaks in your schedule, if you are tired i be harder to retain the material you have been revising.

Here are a few tips for revision techniques

> **Go through your notes and try to summarise them**
>
> **Learn the key cases, as these are essential to know**
>
> **Make sure you understand how the judge has applied the law to the facts so you c the same in an examination scenario**
>
> **If the case is one you may also want to use in an essay, be sure you understan problems it raises or solves and / or the concept of law that is involved**

Example

In **Brown**, the judges decided that consent was not a defence to serious harm, so this would ap a scenario involving GBH.

It raises a problem in the law, because the reasoning was obscure. It was not sufficiently clea the consent defence failed. It could be argued that the defence fails if harm was intended would apply to **s 18** but not **s 20**), or alternatively that the defence fails if harm was seriou would apply to both **s 18** and **s 20**).

Another problem, and one which relates to the concept of fault, is that the acts were consens the element of fault was low but the conviction was for grievous bodily harm. The decision tha were guilty does not appear to satisfy either utilitarianism or distributive justice. The activit place in private, so the burden on the men of a criminal conviction arguably outweighed any benefit in finding such behaviour illegal.

> **Go through the summaries of the topic. These provide a base of the essential points may need to be addressed**
>
> **Go to the examination board's website for past exam papers, mark schemes and rep**
>
> **Practice answering questions then look at the examiners' mark schemes and reports if you were on the right track**

Revision of fault

summary
Note the importance of fault in proving liability and the cases where no fault is required

Remember to consider not only how important fault is in criminal and/or civil law but how far it should be. Remember too that you may need to discuss strict liability, or liability without fault.

Example

Fault is especially important in criminal law, as someone should be found to be at fault before being convicted of a crime. However, in **Harrow LBC v Shah**, it was held that the offence of selling a lottery ticket to a person under 16 was one of strict liability, so a shopkeeper was liable even though he was not present at the time of sale by a member of staff. Although this seems unfair society sees it as important that young people are protected. Strict liability for regulatory crimes like this is not so hard to justify, but in 'real' crimes there is more controversy. This is why in **Sweet v Parsley**, the HL held *mens rea* must always be proved unless Parliament has clearly stated it is a strict liability crime, and this was followed in **B v DPP** to allow an appeal against a conviction for inciting a child of 14 to indecency.

Examination tip

Whichever area you are studying, be sure to relate your cases to the specific question. You will need to do more than explain fault and/or strict liability. You may need to consider how *important* fault is in proving liability. Use cases to support what you say; perhaps some where you feel the outcome was unjust because D had a low level of fault (see Tasks 4, 7, 9 & 10).

Summary of the main points

- The main fault element in criminal law is *mens rea*
- Intention is the highest level of fault
- For most crimes the level of fault is subjective recklessness
- Manslaughter has a lower level of fault and can be committed by 'gross negligence'
- Defences can reduce or even remove the fault element
- Mitigating and aggravating factors indicate higher or lower levels of fault which can thus affect the sentence
- 'State of affairs' crimes do not require any fault at all, D can be liable just for being in the wrong place at the wrong time
- The main fault element in contract is breach of the agreement
- The main fault element in tort is negligence, not reaching the required standard of care
- Professionals have a higher duty, children a lower one (Bolam, Mullins)
- There is an element of fault seen in causation, as this requires foreseeability of harm
- In nuisance the fault element is that D has 'unreasonably interfered' with someone's enjoyment of land
- Motive is not usually relevant in finding liability, but can be in nuisance if malice is shown – Christie v Davy
- Strict liability is liability without fault and applies in both criminal and civil law

Examination tip

Read the question carefully to see where the emphasis lies. Whether you concentrate on criminal civil law you need to focus on what is being asked and not on what you have seen before in papers (though these may be very similar).

When evaluating the law, look at the case examples given in this booklet and also the (especially Tasks 4 and 7, and 9 & 10 below). There are plenty of examples of decisions where liability of D seems to depend not on fault but on the consequence, especially in manslaughter where the level of fault may be low but juries are swayed by the fact that D has caused a death

Essay pointer

When evaluating the importance of fault refer to some of the examples where the level of fault seems too low. In particular, manslaughter cases such as those where D is liable for *failing* to do something, the 'omissions' cases. Failing to do something doesn't seem as bad as actively doing something. In **Pittwood**, the gatekeeper forgot to close the gate and was guilty of manslaughter when someone was killed by a train. There are many other case examples on omissions which can be used to illustrate that a low level of fault may be enough for a manslaughter conviction.

Here are some other points to use in an evaluation of fault

- D may be guilty of murder even if the intent is only to seriously injure – DPP v Smith
- Gross negligence manslaughter has a lower level of fault than such a serious crime warrants
- Unlawful act manslaughter only requires mens rea for the unlawful act and not for the death
- The offences of s 47 ABH, and GBH under s 20, have a lower level of fault than the actus reus suggests e.g., Savage
- The thin-skull rule means D may be liable due to vulnerability in the victim rather than because of fault and this seems harsh (Blaue / Smith v Leech-Brain)
- Proving fault can be difficult in negligence and many victims are left without compensation, especially in medical cases
- The NHS Redress Act which came into force in 2012 addresses some of the problems but is voluntary
- The various tests for duty and breach mean the tort system is inconsistent in providing remedies
- Strict liability allows for liability without fault in both criminal and civil law

Examination tip

Use cases you are familiar with from whatever area of law you have studied to illustrate an answer. Some of the ideas here could also be considered in a discussion of law and justice so make a note of those where you feel justice has not been achieved. This also works both ways so you could mention a theory of justice to argue that a decision or law is wrong. Aristotle argued that the basis of justice is fairness, and finding someone liable without fault can be seen as unfair. It can even be said to be immoral, and therefore against natural law.

Task 9

Find your answers to Task 4 and add an opposing argument to the criticism. This will help you to show a balanced view in an essay. Here are the cases again with a criticism added (so if you haven't done that task please complete it now without peeking).

Criminal case	Criticism
Savage	She did not intend harm so should have been guilty of battery not ABH
Khan & Khan	They should have been guilty of manslaughter as she would not have died if they had sought medical help. They showed more fault than Stone & Dobinson who were found guilty
Clinton	He should have been guilty of murder not manslaughter because he clearly intended to kill her, the highest level of fault
Blaue	He should have been guilty of murder not manslaughter because there was intent to seriously injure which is sufficient fault for murder
Majewski	He did not really know what he was doing and being reckless in getting drunk is not as blameworthy as being reckless as regards the offence
Meah v	He did not know there was caustic soda in the lemonade so should not have been guilty
Harrow LBC v	The shopkeeper did not know his employee had sold the ticket to someone underage so should not have been guilty
Winzar	He did not voluntarily commit any offence, so was not at fault. Therefore he should not have been criminally liable

Task 10

Now do the same for some tort examples, this time based on Task 7.

Tort case	Criticism of the decision
Nettleship v Weston	A learner driver is not as blameworthy as an experienced driver so she should not have been liable
Paris v Stepney BC	The employer would not have been found negligent if the man had two good eyes so it seems unfair that he was found in breach of duty
Mullins v Richard	A 15-year-old should know that rulers could break and cause harm so she showed a sufficient degree of fault for breach of duty
Adams v Ursell	It seems unfair as he was providing a service to the residents and could not be said to be to blame for the natural smells from this service
Belka v Prosperini	The taxi driver should have taken greater care on a busy road. Although C was partly to blame a fairer apportioning of fault would have been 50-50

Task 11: Case study on Orchard v Lee

Read the case of **Orchard v Lee** under the tort of negligence and answer the following questions

What was the primary question for the court?

What does this mean?

What was said to be the correct approach to liability?

In which case was this approach confirmed.

How was age relevant?

Do you think the child was sufficiently blameless to avoid liability?

Examination practice

Although different exam boards have different ways of styling their examination papers, there always going to be common elements. You will need to be able to apply the law you have learnt particular scenario and you will need to be able to evaluate a given topic to provide a critique o law, including reforms where appropriate.

A general guide to examination papers

Read **all** questions carefully before deciding which to answer.

Look again at the ones you wish to answer to make sure you can do so and make brief n This can be a useful checklist later when you are tired and your memory begins to fail.

Structure your answer. A solid start is worth a lot and gets the examiner on your side. A plan is helpful.

It is necessary to do more than regurgitate your notes. Never put in irrelevant materia because you know it – there is **never** a question asking you to 'write all you know about...'. need to be selective as to what is relevant, and choose appropriate cases and examp support of what you say.

In essay questions, you will usually be asked to form an opinion or to weigh up argumen and against a particular statement. Here a broader range of knowledge is needed sh arguments for, arguments against and an evaluation of these arguments. You should a round off your answer with a short concluding paragraph, preferably using some of the wc from the question to indicate to the examiner that you are addressing the specific issue rais

Essays should have a logical structure. The beginning should introduce the subject matte central part should explain / analyse / criticise it as appropriate, and the conclusion should the various strands of argument together with reference to the question set.

Try to consider alternative arguments. A well-rounded essay will bring in other views even disagree with them; you cannot shoot them down without setting them up first.

Here is an idea of how to structure your essay.

Writing a discussion essay: staging the information logically

If you stage your essay as follows, it will make it easy to read, logically structured and easier to It may also mean you don't leave out important points. Here's how it works:

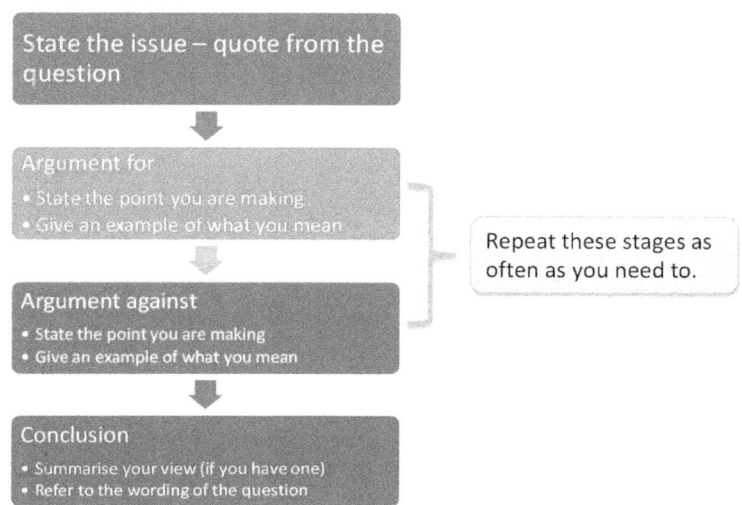

Writing each paragraph: making each one logical and easy to read (and write!)

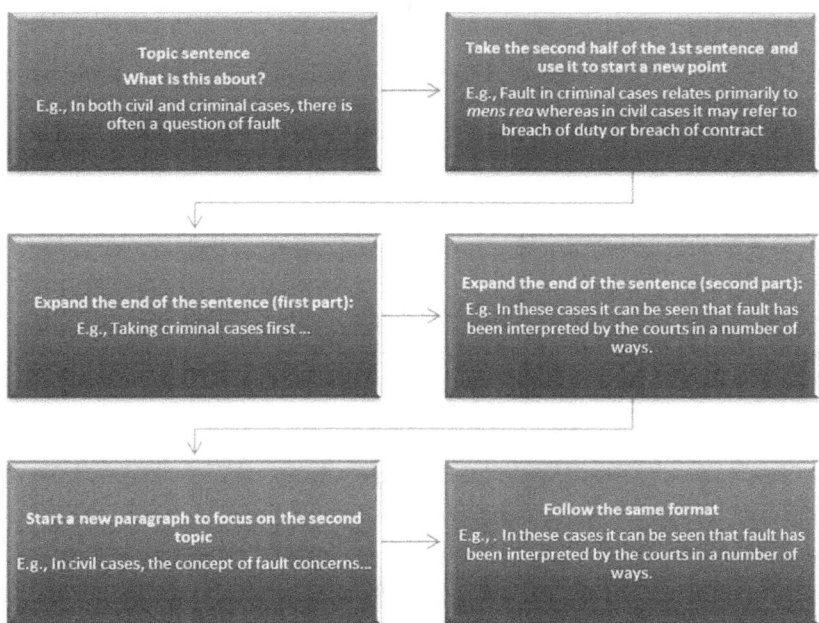

Finally, make sure you cover the whole question; there are only a certain number of marks available. The examiner has a mark scheme to work to, so however brilliant your answer to one part of the question is, missing out the other parts will severely reduce your total marks.

Examination practice for fault

Although different exam boards have different ways of styling their examination papers, there always going to be common elements. You will need to be able to explain and evaluate a g concept to provide a critique of the area, including case examples and reference to theorists wh appropriate.

Examination tip

I cannot say this too often as it is such a regular bug-bear of examiners' reports. There ma similarities in the questions on past papers, but look carefully at the wording to make sure you the emphasis right. You can prepare a basic answer to a question but you will need to be abl adapt it to cover the specific point raised. It is important to make sure you answer the ac question, not the one you hoped to get which you saw in an earlier paper.

The 'Essay pointers' and 'Examination tips' provide you with information to use in an essay. through these and your answers to the tasks before doing the examination practice below.

Task 12: Evaluation practice

As practice in developing a critique of the law, make a few notes to expand on the comme regards the element of fault involved and whether this seems just.

> **The fault level in murder includes an intention to cause grievous bodily harm**
>
> **In Savage, the court confirmed the case of Roberts and held that the fault level (*mens* for ABH is the same as that for assault or battery**
>
> **In the tort of negligence, whether a duty of care is owed is partly based on p considerations**
>
> **The standard of care in negligence is based on what a reasonable person would do, no particular D**
>
> **The rule in Rylands v Fletcher is a tort of strict liability so D is liable for an 'escape' ev great care has been taken**

Examination tip

There are often two parts to an examination question on fault. These cover the 'is' and the 'sh points. Thus you may need to consider not only whether there *is* liability without fault, bu whether there *should* be liability without fault. Alternatively you may be asked whether fa important in assessing liability and then whether it *should* be. Always read the question carefu see what you need to discuss. It is also a good idea to be prepared to argue for and against so the points you raise to show you are taking a balanced view (Tasks 9 & 10 should help with thi always, use case examples to illustrate your points.

Task 13: Examination question

Here is a typical examination question on fault. Read the question carefully and then answer it material from the tasks or choosing your own.

'Briefly explain what is meant by fault. Discuss whether liability does and should always depe proof of fault.'

As always, a logical approach is needed. Here is a basic plan to build on.

Explain the meaning fault (briefly)

Explain the extent to which liability does depend on fault

> This is the 'is' part mentioned earlier (in this case 'does') in the examination tip. Before you can go on to the 'should part' you need show whether liability does depend on fault.
>
> Identify the fault elements in various areas of law, using examples.

Discuss the extent to which liability should always be based on fault

> This is the 'should' part, the evaluation. Here you need to offer a critique of fault-based and non-fault based liability.
>
> Consider the arguments for and against fault-based liability.
>
> Note the 'always' part. There may be times when liability shouldn't 'always' depend on fault, use cases and examples to discuss this.

Bring together your arguments in a brief concluding paragraph.

Answers to self-test questions and tasks

Task 1

You may have different cases but here is a comparison for each area.

The fault element for gross negligence manslaughter is that D was sufficiently negligent for the to be deemed criminal. In **Stone and Dobinson** the Ds had made insufficient efforts to care for sister, and she died from anorexia. They did not have the *mens rea* for murder but were found g of gross negligence manslaughter. They had voluntarily taken on a duty to look after her and v at fault in breaching this duty. In **Wood and Hodgson 2003**, a 10-year-old girl was visiting the She found some ecstasy tablets in a cigarette packet and took some. There was evidence that had hidden the tablets, and they had attempted to treat her, but they did not call an ambulance some time. She later died in hospital. They were charged with gross negligence manslaughter the jury decided they did not have a sufficiently high level of fault, they were not *grossly* neglig and so they were not guilty.

The fault element for civil negligence is breach of duty. In **Bolton v Stone**, the club had t precautions by putting up a high fence, and also the risk was very low as it happened so ra There was a no breach of duty, so they were not liable. In **Paris v Stepney BC**, the employer k the worker was already blind in one eye so he should have taken greater care by making him goggles. Here the fault was greater because of this knowledge, and because of the fact that it w have been cheap and easy to avoid the risk. He had breached his duty and was liable.

Task 2

The answer depends on your choice of cases but an example would be **Cunningham**. The element was subjective recklessness and the prosecution failed to prove that D was awar actions might cause harm. The effect was that he had no *mens rea* so was not guilty. Other examples are shown above in Task 1.

Task 3

Here are two examples.

Intoxication: In **Kingston**, the court said that if the defendant is involuntarily intoxicated and ca form the *mens rea* of intent there may be no liability, because there is no blameworthiness inv which is fair because D lacks fault, usually a requirement for criminal liability. Howeve **Majewski**, the court held that if intoxication is voluntary the defendant is seen as at fa becoming intoxicated, so will be deemed reckless and so have *mens rea* for any crimes req recklessness rather than intent. This does not seem fair because being reckless in getting dr not the same as being reckless in the committing of a crime.

Automatism: This defence is available where the defendant is not at fault at all. It is a de where the defendant has no control over the act committed. In **Hill v Baxter**, the court g hypothetical example of losing control of a car after being attacked by a swarm of bees. A succ plea of automatism results in an acquittal, showing that the law recognises that a defendant h blameworthiness at all, and this seems fair as the action cannot be said to be voluntary. Howe there is some control then an element of fault remains. This was the case in **Attorney-Gen reference (No 2 of 1992)**, where he was partly in control of his actions so the defence failed. H therefore liable for the result of his actions. As he was partly in control of his actions it can b he was acting voluntarily, it is also arguable that he was at fault for driving so long, so this is fai

Task 4

Criminal case	Criticism
Savage	She did not intend harm so should have been guilty of battery not ABH
Khan & Khan	They should have been guilty of manslaughter as she would not have died if they had sought medical help. They showed more fault than Stone & Dobinson who were found guilty
Clinton	He should have been guilty of murder not manslaughter because he clearly intended to kill her, the highest level of fault
Blaue	He should have been guilty of murder not manslaughter because there was intent to seriously injure which is sufficient fault for murder
Majewski	He did not really know what he was doing and being reckless in getting drunk is not as blameworthy as being reckless as regards the offence
Meah v	He did not know there was caustic soda in the lemonade so should not have been guilty
Harrow LBC v	The shopkeeper did not know his employee had sold the ticket to someone underage so should not have been guilty
Winzar	He did not voluntarily commit any offence, so was not at fault. Therefore he should not have been criminally liable

Task 5

The answer depends on your choice of cases but a tort example would be **Bolton v Stone**. The fault element for negligence is not acting as a reasonable person would. The cricket club had taken precautions and the risk was low, so C could not prove they had breached their duty of care. The effect was that they had not been negligent and were not liable to pay compensation. In **Donoghue v Stevenson**, the manufacture was at fault in not keeping the bottles clean and free from snails. In this case there was a breach of duty and the manufacturer was liable. In contract law, the case of **Super Servant II** shows that a contract will not be frustrated where a party is at fault. They knew they could not provide a ship as they had leased it elsewhere, so the effect was that the contract was not frustrated by the fact that they were unable to fulfil it. That was their fault.

Task 6

Here are two possibilities.

Contributory negligence: In **Gannon v Rotherham MBC**, the court held that a 14-year-old ought to recognise the danger of diving into the shallow end of a pool, so he was partly at fault and was held to have contributed to his own injuries. The effect of this defence was that D was liable but damages were reduced to reflect the fact that C was partly to blame.

Consent: In **Ratcliff v McConnell**, on similar facts to the above case, a 19-year-old student was seriously injured when diving into a swimming pool. He had been drinking and so was sufficiently at fault to be seen to have consented to the risk of harm. The effect of this defence was that the college was not liable at all.

Task 7

Tort case	Criticism of the decision
Nettleship v Weston	A learner driver is not as blameworthy as an experienced driver so she should not have been liable
Paris v Stepney BC	The employer would not have been found negligent if the man had two good eyes so it seems unfair that he was found in breach of duty
Mullins v Richard	A 15-year-old should know that rulers could break and cause harm so she showed a sufficient degree of fault for breach of duty
Adams v Ursell	It seems unfair as he was providing a service to the residents and could not be said to be to blame for the natural smells from this service
Belka v Prosperini	The taxi driver should have taken greater care on a busy road. Although C was partly to blame a fairer apportioning of fault would have been 50-50

Task 8

Under the **Consumer Protection Act** there is no need to prove fault. C only needs to show th manufacturer is a producer as defined in **s 1 (2)**, and that the product was defective, or unsafe is different to proving negligence under **Donoghue v Stevenson**, where there is a need to pr was in breach of duty, the fault element for negligence. On the facts of **Donoghue** the manufa would be liable in negligence and under the Act because he had allowed the bottles to be contaminated. The difference under the Act is that even if he had taken great care to everything clean, but somehow a snail had still ended up in a bottle, he would have been liabl though not at fault. It would be enough that the product (the beer) contained a defect (the sn

Self-test questions

> Fault is proved in civil law by showing that someone has breached their duty of care (tort) failed to meet their contractual obligations (contract). For criminal law fault is sho proving mens rea, i.e., being reckless or acting with intent
>
> Criminal defences such as diminished responsibility and insanity show a reduced level of that D is not fully responsible. Automatism shows no fault at all as D has no control over committed. Duress and self-defence show a reduced level of fault, although they excuse than remove the fault element. The civil defence of act of God or act of a stranger indica not at fault in any way. The defence of contributory negligence shows D is not wholly and damages are reduced to reflect the amount that C is at fault
>
> This depends on which case you chose. A criminal example is **Gemmell & Richards** wh young boys did not recognise the risk of their actions in setting light to some papers s was no liability. A civil example is **Latimer v AEC** where the factory owner had done all th reasonable in the circumstances
>
> The answer depends on your chosen cases but an example is **Meah v Roberts**. This c used to support an argument for imposing strict liability because it makes people care protects the consumer. The same case can be used to support an argument for not in

strict liability as the man who served it was not at fault. He did not know the caustic soda was in the lemonade so should not have criminal liability

Fault may have an effect on sentencing because aggravating and mitigating factors are taken into account. These factors can indicate a higher or lower amount of fault, and a judge will try to find a sentence which fits the blameworthiness of D

The rule that children are judged against a child of similar age rather than a reasonable adult recognises that children are less likely to see the risk of harm and so are not at fault to the same degree as an adult would be

The breach factors affect fault in negligence because they are used to decide whether D has reached a reasonable standard of care. If D has done all that is expected of the reasonable person to avoid the risk of harm, then there is insufficient fault for liability

The defence of contributory negligence reflects the degree of fault involved by as it gives the judge discretion to apportion damages in accordance with the amount that C is also at fault

Task 9

Criminal case	Criticism	Alternative argument
Savage	She did not intend harm so should have been guilty of battery not ABH	Someone was hurt because of her actions and she intended an aggressive act (throwing the beer) so there was sufficient fault for her to be guilty of ABH
Khan & Khan	They should have been guilty of manslaughter as she would not have died if they had sought medical help. They showed more fault than Stone & Dobinson who were found guilty	This is harder to find an alternative argument for but the court felt it was not in the public interest for a drug-dealer to owe a duty to a client so this would be one counter-argument
Clinton	He should have been guilty of murder not manslaughter because he clearly intended to kill her, the highest level of fault	He was not a danger to society, only his wife, and it was partly her fault that he lost control so a manslaughter verdict was correct
Blaue	He should have been guilty of murder not manslaughter because there was intent to seriously injure which is sufficient fault for murder	The thin-skull rule is unfair. She would not have died without her religion so it was not his fault she died. He should not have been guilty for the death, only GBH
Majewski	He did not really know what he was doing and being reckless in getting drunk is not as blameworthy as being reckless as regards the offence	He was at fault for getting drunk and so aggressive, so a conviction was fair
Meah v Roberts	He did not know there was caustic soda in the lemonade so should not have been guilty	This could have caused serious harm so strict liability is right here as it should make people more careful in future
Harrow LBC v Shah	The shopkeeper did not know his employee had sold the ticket to someone underage so should not have been guilty	No real harm can come of a child buying a lottery ticket so strict liability is not justified
Winzar	He did not voluntarily commit any offence, so was not at fault. Therefore he should not have been criminally liable	He was drunk and so arguably had mens rea as he was reckless in getting drunk (as decided in Majewski)

Task 10

Tort case	Criticism of the decision	Alternative argument
Nettleship v Weston	A learner driver is not as blameworthy as an experienced driver so she should not have been liable	Road users need protecting from all drivers and she should have been more careful
Paris v Stepney BC	The employer would not have been found negligent if the man had two good eyes so it seems unfair that he was found in breach of duty	An employer should take care of the safety of all employees and he knew the man was partially blind so was fully at fault in not supplying goggles
Mullins v Richard	A 15-year-old should know that rulers could break and cause harm so she showed a sufficient degree of fault for breach of duty	Children, even at 15, are less at fault than an adult would be as they have less life experience
Adams v Ursell	It seems unfair as he was providing a service to the residents and could not be said to be to blame for the natural smells from this service	The decision was right because even though the level of fault was low it still caused a nuisance to those living nearby
Belka v Prosperini	The taxi driver should have taken greater care on a busy road. Although C was partly to blame a fairer apportioning of fault would have been 50-50	The decision was correct because C was drunk and chose to run across the road, so had a greater level of fault than the driver

Task 11: Case study on Orchard v Lee

The primary question for the court was whether the conduct of the child was culpable

This means was the child blameworthy, or sufficiently at fault

The correct approach to liability was that for a child to be held culpable the conduct be careless to a very high degree,

This approach was confirmed in Mullins v Richards

Age was relevant because the standard of care owed was measured against what cou expected as reasonable for a child of the same age

Whether the child was sufficiently blameless to avoid liability is arguable either Children do not see risks as clearly as an adult so should not be expected to take such to avoid them. On the other hand someone was injured and he should have looked v he was going so there was a certain degree of fault involved. On balance I would with the decision that he was not liable as the level of fault was low

Task 12

The fault level in murder includes an intention to cause grievous bodily harm	This seems unjust because the law is treating defendants with different levels of fault in the same way. An intention to kill is a much higher level of fault than an intention to cause grievous bodily harm but both result in a murder conviction. As murder has a mandatory sentence of life imprisonment D will get a life sentence whether there was intent to kill or intent to cause serious harm and this also seems unjust because the fault element is different but this difference cannot be taken into account at the sentencing stage
In Savage the court confirmed the case of Roberts and held that the fault level (mens rea) for ABH is the same as that for assault or battery	This seems unjust because mens rea should match the actus reus so that D is only liable for the act intended or foreseen, in this case a battery. It seems wrong that a person can be convicted of a more serious offence than the one intended
In the tort of negligence, whether a duty of care is owed is partly based on policy considerations	In some ways this is just because where the claim is against a public body such as the fire brigade (as in Watts v Herts CC) any compensation would come from the public (taxpayers) and any payment of damages will reduce funds for the particular public body to spend elsewhere. On the other hand if the court finds it is not fair, just and reasonable to impose a duty this leaves C with no compensation for any injuries suffered. Another criticism is that cases based on such policy considerations can lead to inconsistent decisions. Justice cannot be achieved if the law is inconsistent
The standard of care in negligence is based on what a reasonable person would do, not the particular D	This seems unjust at times because it can lead to finding liability where there is little fault, as in Nettleship v Weston. However the courts do look at the fault element fairly in some cases, as in Orchard v Lee where the child's conduct was measured against what would be expected of another child of the same age, rather than a reasonable adult
The rule in Rylands v Fletcher is a tort of strict liability so D is liable for an 'escape' even if great care has been taken	Although this seems unjust at first there is another part of the rule that says the thing that escapes must be 'dangerous' and 'likely to do mischief'. If you have something dangerous on your land it is right that you should be liable if it escapes and harms someone

Task 13 Examination question

There is no 'right' answer to evaluation questions and many different approaches, so this is only a guide to what could be included. Your answer should include something on the following though.

Consideration of whether fault is important

Reference to cases of strict or absolute liability, where there is no fault

Reference to cases which did not seem fair to show liability should depend on fault

Reference to other cases which you think were just, to show liability should not 'always' depend on fault but maybe only 'sometimes'

Reference to the word 'always' in your conclusion

This answer contains a comprehensive range of examples and criticisms. You can't cover everything that is here so choose the ones you feel you would be able to explain most competently. The wider your range of examples the less depth you need, as long as you remember to evaluate as well as explain. I have left out some of the material in the essay pointers, which you could use instead of or to supplement the points below. Where I have used the answers to tasks in the evaluation pa have noted these in brackets. I have only used criminal law, so if you include the civil law you w certainly need to reduce the number of examples (a brief guide is given at the end of this answer

Start with a brief explanation of the general meaning of fault in terms of blameworthir culpability and/or responsibility for one's actions

Go on to identify the fault elements in various areas of law

Mens rea is the main element of fault in criminal law

Explain

There are different levels of fault seen in the *mens rea* of a crime

Intent is the highest level of fault, but can be indirect

The fault level in murder includes an intention to cause grievous bodily harm

Subjective recklessness is a higher level of fault than objective recklessness

Gross negligence is the fault element for manslaughter; this is a low level of fault

Unlawful act manslaughter only requires MR for the unlawful act, not a death

Strict liability cases involve no *mens rea*

Evaluate

The **Nedrick** test for murder is too close to subjective recklessness, e.g. in, **Matthews Alleyne** they were guilty of murder because they knew he couldn't swim, which display fault than a direct intent to kill someone.

Including intention to cause grievous bodily harm seems unjust because the law is tre defendants with different levels of fault in the same way. An intention to kill is a higher level of fault than an intention to cause grievous bodily harm but both resul murder conviction. As murder has a mandatory sentence of life imprisonment D will life sentence whether there was intent to kill or intent to cause serious harm and thi seems unjust because the fault element is different but this difference cannot be take account at the sentencing stage (**Task 12**).

The HL recognised objective recklessness was too low a level of fault for criminal li (**Gemmell and Richards** overruled **Caldwell**).

Savage or **Roberts** illustrate the problem with the fault element for ABH. In **Savage**, s not intend harm so should have been guilty of battery not ABH. However, someon hurt because of her actions and she intended an aggressive act (throwing the be arguably there was sufficient fault for her to be guilty of ABH (**Tasks 4 and 9**).

The fact that the *mens rea* for ABH is the same as that for assault or battery seems un feel the MR should match the *actus reus* so that D is only liable for the act intenc foreseen, in this case a battery. It seems wrong that a person can be convicted of a serious offence than the one intended (**Task 12**). On balance, I think the *mens rea* fc should be intention or recklessness to cause at least some harm.

The cases on gross negligence manslaughter sometimes conflict. In **Stone and Dot** the Ds had made insufficient efforts to care for his sister, and she died from anorexia did not have the *mens rea* for murder but were found guilty of gross negl manslaughter. They had voluntarily taken on a duty to look after her and were at f breaching this duty. In **Wood and Hodgson 2003**, a 10-year-old girl was visiting the Ds. She found some ecstasy tablets in a cigarette packet and took some. There was evidence that they had hidden the tablets, and they had attempted to treat her, but they did not call an ambulance for some time. She later died in hospital. They were charged with gross negligence manslaughter but the jury decided they did not have a sufficiently high level of fault, they were not *grossly* negligent, and so they were not guilty (**Task 1**).

The MR for unlawful act manslaughter should at least be recklessness as to the death. It is not fair that someone can be liable for a death when, e.g., only being reckless as to criminal damage, as in **Nedrick**.

There are arguments for and against strict liability. It can be justified for certain regulatory crimes such as minor traffic offences, or when used to protect the public, as in **Meah v Roberts**, where serious harm could have occurred. Imposing strict liability should make people more careful. However, the **Shah** case can be criticised because no real harm can come of a young person buying a lottery ticket so strict liability is not justified (**Tasks 4 and 9**).

Another advantage of liability without fault is that court time and costs are saved because there is no need to prove *mens rea*. However there is less justification for this in real crimes, hence the decision to overturn the convictions in **Sweet v Parsley** and **B v DPP 2000**. On balance I feel serious crimes should always depend on proof of fault.

Actus reus also includes an element of fault

Explain

Actus reus must be voluntary e.g., **Leicester v Pearson**

Absolute liability cases involve no fault at all

D is not usually liable for an omission to act, unless there is a duty of care

The thin-skull rule means D can be liable for unforeseen consequences e.g., **Blaue**

Evaluate

The case of **Winzar** can be compared to **Leicester v Pearson** and illustrates that there is not always a requirement of fault, which may be unfair. The injustice of the decision provides a strong argument against imposing liability without fault. He did not voluntarily commit any offence, so was not at fault. Therefore he should not have been criminally liable (**Tasks 4 and 9**).

Discuss duty of care cases e.g., **Pittwood/Stone & Dobinson** but compare to **Khan** (**Tasks 1, 4 and 9**).

In **Khan**, they should have been guilty of manslaughter as she would not have died if they had sought medical help, which would have been easy. They showed more fault than the Ds in **Pittwood** and **Stone & Dobinson** who were all found guilty, but who were more thoughtless than criminally negligent.

The thin-skull rule is unfair. In **Blaue**, she would not have died with treatment so it was not his fault she died. He should not have been guilty for the death, only GBH. On the other hand it could be argued that he should have been guilty of murder not manslaughter because there was intent to seriously injure which is sufficient fault for murder (**Tasks 4 and 9**).

Defences (both full and partial) may show a lower level of fault.

Explain

Automatism defence shows complete lack of fault as described in **Hill v Baxter**

Loss of control and diminished responsibility show reduced fault as in **Clinton** and **Frean**

Intoxication shows a high level of fault so usually fails

Evaluate

The defence of automatism is available where the defendant is not at fault at all. It defence where the defendant has no control over the act committed. In **Hill v Baxter** court gave a hypothetical example of losing control of a car after being attacked by a sw of bees. A successful plea of automatism results in an acquittal, showing that the recognises that a defendant has no blameworthiness at all, and this seems fair as the a cannot be said to be voluntary. However, if there is some control then an element of remains. This was the case in **Attorney-General's reference (No 2 of 1992)**, where he partly in control of his actions so was found to be at fault. He was therefore liable fo result of his actions and the defence failed. As he was partly in control of it can be sa was acting voluntarily and also he could be seen to be at fault for driving so long so t fair **(Task 3)**.

In **Kingston**, the court said that if the defendant is involuntarily intoxicated and cannot the *mens rea* of intent there may be no liability, because there is no blameworth involved, which is fair because D lacks fault, usually a requirement in criminal law. How in **Majewski**, the court held that if intoxication is voluntary the defendant is seen as at in becoming intoxicated, so will be deemed reckless and so have *mens rea* for any c requiring recklessness rather than intent. This does not seem fair because being reckl getting drunk is not the same as being reckless in the committing of a crime (Ta Majewski did not really know what he was doing and being reckless in getting drunk is blameworthy as being reckless as regards the offence **(Tasks 4 and 9)**.

In **Clinton** he should have been guilty of murder not manslaughter because he c intended to kill her, the highest level of fault. On the other hand he was not a dan society, only his wife, and it was partly her fault that he lost control so a manslat verdict was correct **(Tasks 4 and 9)**.

The sentencing stage also relates to fault.

Explain

The judge can take into account the level of fault at the time of the crime by looking at aggra and mitigating factors.

Evaluate

Even if D is convicted of a crime without proof of fault, the judge can take any lack of fau account as a mitigating factor and so give a lighter sentence.

There is a problem with the mandatory life sentence for murder, however, because the judge take into account any lack of moral fault, e.g., in a euthanasia case **(Inglis)**.

Conclusion

Where a person may not only have a criminal conviction, but may also get a prison sente seems right that liability should *always* depend on fault, especially in criminal law. However, be seen above, there are often arguments on both sides. This highlights the fact that althoug *should* usually be a requirement of fault, this is not *always* the case and strict liability is sometimes justified to protect the public, as in **Meah**.

However, for serious crimes, I feel that fault should *always* be proved and should fit the *actus reus*. Thus liability for murder should depend on proving intent to kill, liability for GBH should depend on proof of intent or recklessness to cause serious harm and for ABH to cause some harm, unlike in **Savage**. On balance, although there are a few circumstances in which it is acceptable to find liability without fault I feel there should almost *always* be an element of fault before someone is found liable.

Note the use of the word 'always' in the conclusion. This shows you are responding to the specific point in the question (I have put it in italics merely to highlight it, you needn't do this)

Alternative answer

If you use civil law you would have a similar plan. Here is a brief guide plus reference to the relevant tasks.

Explain the fault element in civil law using examples

Breach is the fault element in contract

Breach of a duty of care is the fault element in negligence and under the **Occupiers' Liability Act**

Unreasonableness is the fault element in nuisance

Provide examples of **strict liability to show that there is not** *always* **a requirement of fault, e.g.:**

    Consumer Protection Act

    Rylands v Fletcher

    Vicarious liability

Evaluate

Examples for each of the above points, to illustrate the requirement of fault in civil law

Fault element (**Tasks 5, 8 and 11**)

Discuss defences, e.g., contributory negligence reflects the fact that C is also blameworthy. Blame can therefore be apportioned by the judge when deciding on the remedy (**Task 6**)

Discuss remedies (damages and injunctions) where the judge can take into account the level of fault

Discuss whether liability should always depend on proof of fault, referring to examples (**Tasks 7, 10 and 12**)

Add a little on vicarious liability. .Fault must still be proved (against the employee who was negligent) but the employer is the one who pays even though not personally at fault

Produce arguments for and against imposing fault (see table under 'Liability without fault' plus **Tasks 8, 10 and 12**)

Discuss **Pearson** report and alternative schemes

Conclusion

'It can be argued that strict liability is sometimes desirable, particularly in areas where there is a need to protect the public. There is also occasionally justification for making, e.g., an employer vicariously liable for an employee or a business strictly liable for harm to consumers, as under the **Consumer Protection Act**, because employers and businesses are usually in a better position to pay compensation. Therefore liability should not *always* depend on fault. However, on balance e though liability should not *always* depend on fault I believe the arguments for fault-based liab are more compelling and should be the general rule'.

Appendix: Abbreviations and acknowledgements

The following abbreviations are commonly used. You may use them in an examination answer, but write them in full the first time, e.g., write 'actual bodily harm (ABH)' and then after that you can just write 'ABH'.

General

Draft Code – A Criminal Code for England and Wales (Law Commission No. 177), 1989

CCRC Criminal Cases Review Commission

ABH actual bodily harm

GBH grievous bodily harm

D defendant

C claimant

V Victim

CA Court of Appeal

HL House of Lords

SC Supreme Court

Acts

S – section (thus **s 1** Theft Act 1968 refers to section 1 of that Act)

s 1(2) means section 1 subsection 2 of an Act.

OAPA – Offences against the Person Act 1861

In cases – these don't need to be written in full

CC (at beginning) chief constable

CC (at end) county council

BC borough council

DC district council

LBC London borough council

AHA Area Health Authority

J Justice

LJ Lord Justice

LCJ Lord Chief Justice

LC Lord Chancellor

AG Attorney General

CPS Crown Prosecution Service

DPP Director of Public Prosecutions

AG Attorney General

www.ingramcontent.com/pod-product-compliance
Lightning Source LLC
Chambersburg PA
CBHW070723180526
45167CB00004B/1591